NATURE'S GROSSEST

SKUNK STENCH

By Kate Shoemaker

Gareth Stevens
PUBLISHING

Please visit our website, www.garethstevens.com. For a free color catalog of all our high-quality books, call toll free 1-800-542-2595 or fax 1-877-542-2596.

Library of Congress Cataloging-in-Publication Data

Shoemaker, Kate.
Skunk stench / by Kate Shoemaker.
p. cm. — (Nature's grossest)
Includes index.
ISBN 978-1-4824-1850-7 (pbk.)
ISBN 978-1-4824-1849-1 (6-pack)
ISBN 978-1-4824-1851-4 (library binding)
1. Skunks — Juvenile literature. I. Title.
QL737.C25 S56 2015
599.76—d23

Published in 2015 by
Gareth Stevens Publishing
111 East 14th Street, Suite 349
New York, NY 10003

Copyright © 2015 Gareth Stevens Publishing

Designer: Katelyn E. Reynolds
Editor: Therese Shea

Photo credits: Cover, p. 1 Tom Brakefield/Stockbyte/Getty Images; pp. 3–24 (background) Oleksii Natykach/Shutterstock.com; pp. 5, 7, 11 Critterbiz/Shutterstock.com; p. 9 Daniel J. Cox/Oxford Scientific/Getty Images; p. 13 (great horned owl) Pictureguy/Shutterstock.com; p. 13 (skunk) Geoffrey Kuchera/Shutterstock.com; p. 15 Holly Kuchera/Shutterstock.com; p. 17 worldswildlifewonders/Shutterstock.com; p. 19 (inset) Dorling Kindersley/Getty Images; p. 19 (main) Rick & Nora Bowers/Visuals Unlimited, Inc./Getty Images; p. 21 Heiko Kiera/Shutterstock.com.

Printed in the United States of America

CPSIA compliance information: Batch #CW15GS: For further information contact Gareth Stevens, New York, New York at 1-800-542-2595.

CONTENTS

Boldface words appear in the glossary.

Hold Your Nose

What's the worst thing you've ever smelled? Stinky socks? Rotten eggs? A skunk can make a **stench** worse than both of these. It might be the worst smell in nature! Read on to find out how and why skunks make this smell.

A Defense

Skunks aren't smelly animals themselves. However, they have special body parts called glands under the base of their tail. These glands make a stinky liquid that gives off the famous skunk stench. A skunk **sprays** this liquid as a **defense**.

6

Ready, Aim, Fire!

A skunk doesn't just spray anywhere. It can actually aim at an enemy. If the enemy is close, the skunk aims at its face and **squirts** its stinky liquid. A skunk can also make a cloud of stink as it's running away.

Predators

Foxes, **bobcats**, dogs, and **coyotes** hunt skunks. However, these predators have a very good sense of smell. That means a skunk's powerful spray smells even worse to them. If they're sprayed once, they may not ever attack another skunk.

Owls and hawks attack skunks from the air. This means that they can catch a skunk by surprise. Some kinds of owls and hawks don't have a good sense of smell. A skunk's spray doesn't bother them.

Warning Signs

Skunks often try to scare off their predators before they spray. They may face the animal, hiss, and show their teeth. They may stamp their feet, too. If all this doesn't scare off predators, it's time to spray.

Skunk Species

There are 11 species, or kinds, of skunks. Each makes a different smell, but all are very powerful. The different species have different markings. The most famous is the striped skunk. It's black with a white "V" shape on its back.

The stink badger is a skunk that pretends to be dead when a predator is near. When the predator gets close, it fires its spray. Spotted skunks do a handstand when they're about to spray! They're shown on the next page. Spotted skunks are also the only skunks that can climb.

Watch Out!

Skunks may spray people, too.
Skunks sometimes walk into
yards looking for food. If you see
the black and white markings
of a skunk, don't get too close.
Slowly move away, and hope it
doesn't spray!

GLOSSARY

bobcat: a wild cat of North America

coyote: a meat-eating animal similar to but smaller than a wolf

defense: a way of guarding against an enemy

spray: to put out a liquid in the form of tiny drops. Also, a cloud of tiny liquid drops.

squirt: to force something out of a little opening in a quick stream

stench: a really gross smell

FOR MORE INFORMATION

BOOKS

Brandon, Taylor. *The Skunk Who Didn't Want to Stink!* Santa Monica, CA: Upside Down Ink, 2011.

Owen, Ruth. *Skunk Kits.* New York, NY: Bearport Publishing, 2011.

Roza, Greg. *Phew! The Skunk and Other Stinky Animals.* New York, NY: PowerKids Press, 2011.

WEBSITES

Skunk
animals.nationalgeographic.com/animals/mammals/skunk/
Want to hear what a skunk sounds like? Check out this site.

Striped Skunk
www.nhptv.org/natureworks/stripedskunk.htm
Learn more about striped skunks and where they live.

INDEX